Reality Is a Skill

Attention Shapes What Becomes Real

Reality Is a Skill

Attention Shapes What Becomes Real

By Oliver C McElroy

An Owl House Book

Published by Owl House Press

RealityIsaSkill.com

ISBN: 979-8-234-08448-4

First edition
Printed in the United States of America

Table of Contents

A Few Words of Warning

Before you go any further, there is something you should know:

Reading this book changes you.

The words and ideas you will encounter within point the mind towards a fundamental shift.

Some things—once truly seen—refuse to return to invisibility.

All of a sudden—things may begin to feel less certain.

Simply because you are seeing more of what is already happening.

If you choose to continue,

approach with curiosity—and a hint of caution.

Some ideas can be discussed without experiencing them.

These are not those ideas.

Know that to read some books is to embrace irreversible change.

Preface

Most people think perception is passive.
That the world appears—and they experience it.

That what they see is what's there.
That what they feel reflects what's happening.
That what they remember is what occurred.

This book takes a different position:

What your nervous system is showing you is not reality.

You experience reality as a synthesis of many processes.
Perception is merely the starting place—the proverbial tip of the iceberg.

This book is not about dismantling that system, but rather about understanding it.
Only then can you begin to work with it.

What follows is not theory.
Each chapter contains something you experience directly.
To allow you to convince yourself.

I do not seek to introduce you to a different reality.
I simply invite you to a different relationship with the one you already have.

CHAPTER 1:

THE FIRST FRACTURE

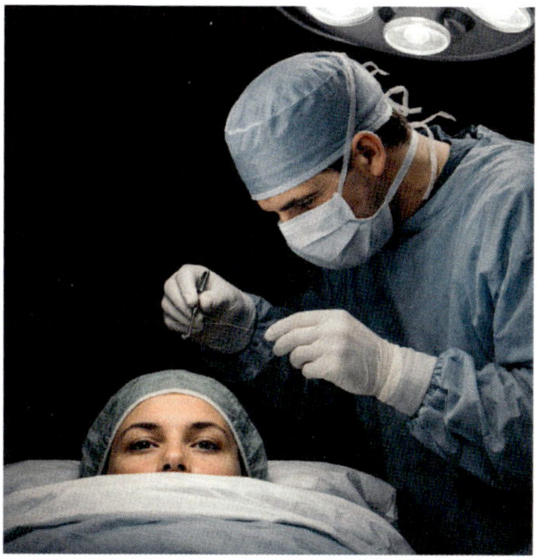

Well, you've probably experienced this. You're walking through a parking lot, or down a grocery store aisle, or across some forgettable stretch of sidewalk that exists only to connect two places that matter more—and then suddenly someone is just... there.

Not approaching. Not arriving.
Just there.

Simply appearing out of nowhere. Close enough to startle you. Close enough that your body reacts before your mind catches up. For a split second, it feels like reality glitched.
You might laugh it off.
You might say, "Oh—I didn't see you."

But that's not quite true.

It's not that you didn't see them.
For a moment, they weren't available to be seen.

There is a place in your vision where the world does not exist.
Not philosophically. Biologically.
A literal hole.

And what's strange isn't that the hole is there.
What's strange is that you've never noticed it.

Your brain has been covering it up your entire life.

Check this out.

Hold this page at arm's length.

Close your left eye. Focus on the plus sign.

Now slowly bring the page closer to your face.

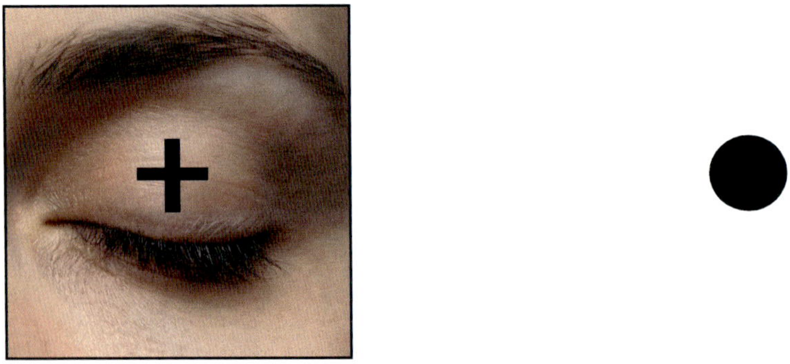

There's a moment—
somewhere in the middle of that movement—
when the black dot disappears.

Not fades.

Not shifts.

It just stops existing.

Nothing on the page changed.

The dot is still there.

You moved. That was enough.

At that distance, the image of the dot falls onto a part of your eye that can't detect it. Instead of showing you a gap, your brain fills it in using the surrounding information.

The result is so seamless that, until now, you had no idea anything was missing...

What you see is not the world as it is.

Your nervous system is actively shaping what you see.

Right now, it is deleting information, filling in gaps, and presenting a seamless result.

If your mind can erase something this obvious...
What else is it not showing you?

The answer is not philosophical.
It is operational.
And it can be trained.

Reality is not what you are given.

Reality is what you learn to perceive.

CHAPTER 2:

THE SKIPPING SECOND

Ever glance at a clock—on a wall or a stove—and notice, for just an instant, that something feels off?
The second hand seems to hesitate, lingering longer than it should, as if time itself briefly stalled before continuing on.

It's easy to dismiss, and most people do.
They assume it's a quirk of the clock or a delay in their own attention catching up to what they're seeing.

But if you pay attention, you'll notice a pattern.
It only happens when you first look.

Try this.

Find a clock with a second hand.
An analog wall clock with a second hand works best.

Look away from it completely and let your gaze settle somewhere else.

Then quickly shift your eyes back to the clock and pay close attention to the very first second you perceive.

It will feel longer than it should.

Even though nothing about the clock has changed.

The movement is consistent and the second hand is not hesitating just for you.

Your eyes don't move smoothly.

They jump.

If you were aware of this, the world would feel unstable because every glance would introduce blurry gaps.

When your gaze lands on the clock, your brain stitches over the gap and extends the first moment you see, resulting in what you felt—that stretched second.

It didn't happen in the clock.

It happened inside you.

You didn't miss a second.

You experienced one that never happened.

CHAPTER 3:

WHERE ARE YOU?

Feel into the moment, when two parts of your body touch and it feels like a single event.
But it isn't.

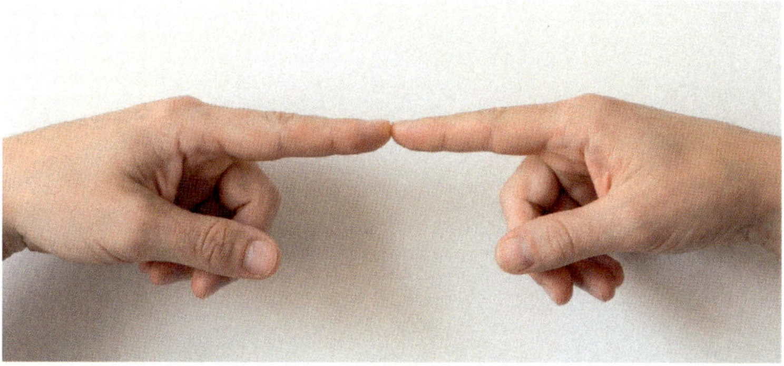

Try this.

Hold your hands in front of you and gently press your two index fingers together. Not hard—just enough to feel clear contact.

Now place your attention in your right finger.
Notice the sensation there—the pressure, the point of contact, the subtle feedback.
Stay with it.

It begins to feel as if your right finger is the one doing the touching. As if your sense of "you" has shifted slightly to that side. As if the left finger is the one being touched.

Now, keep your hands still, and shift your attention to your left finger. The sense of contact reorganizes. Sensation reverses.
Even though nothing about your body changed, your experience shifted.

Shift your focus between your fingers.

The distinction becomes less clear. Not gone.
But harder to pin down. The system feels stable.
But it isn't.

Now you are discovering that the center of your experience is not fixed. It follows attention. And attention is always moving.

You think you're located somewhere specific—behind your eyes, inside your head, looking out at the world.
But that's just where your attention usually rests.

Where attention goes, sensation becomes vivid, and everything else recedes.
You don't notice what fades.
You only notice what lights up.

You call that background. You call that nothing.
But it's still there.

You just aren't.

CHAPTER 4:
BEFORE YOU SEE

I wondre wehn yu wil relize tha yo ar wher yor attention si.

Only part of what you read was actually there.
But it didn't matter. You understood it anyway.

You didn't read every letter.
And yet—you didn't slow down.

You didn't stop to decode it.

You just... read it.

Your eyes took in something incomplete.
Your brain supplied the rest.

It does it immediately, seamlessly. This isn't a trick.
It's how you work.

You don't start with data.
You start with a guess. A prediction.

And what you experience as perception is what happens when that prediction meets input. If they match, the system feels smooth. If they don't, something catches.

But most of the time—you never notice the difference.
You assume you're looking at the world and then interpreting it.
But the sequence is reversed.

And once something is confirmed—it feels obvious.

Stable.

Real.

That's why you can read a sentence with missing letters.
That's why the world feels consistent.

Not because it is.

But because your system is very good at making it feel that way.

And if your perception is being guided—quietly, constantly—by what you expect to see...

Then expectation is not passive.

It's active.

It shapes what appears.

It filters what doesn't.

It fills in what's missing.

So the question isn't whether expectation is influencing your perception.

It is.

The question is—

How much of what you're seeing is actually there?

And how much of it was already decided?

Most people live in the default mode.

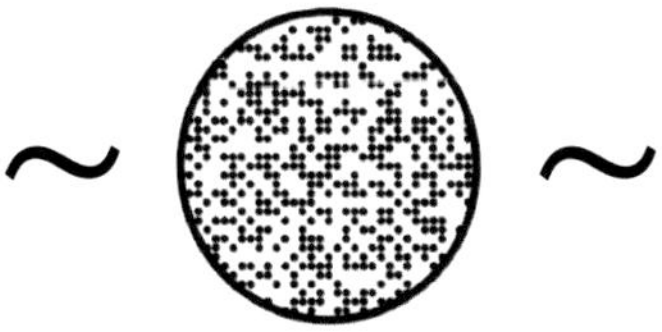

CHAPTER 5:

WHAT YOU BROUGHT

Usually, something arrives before you do.

Before the conversation begins. Before you walk into the room. Before you look at the face in front of you—something has already landed. You assume you're responding to what's there.

But you're not.

Most of the time you're responding to what's there plus what you brought with you—and the two are so entangled that they feel like one thing.

Which means two people can look at exactly the same thing and have completely different experiences. Not different opinions. Different experiences—as if they aren't seeing the same thing at all.

This isn't a metaphor.

Check this out.

Look at the man in this photograph. Take a moment and really look. Notice what thoughts or feelings arise naturally.

Hold this idea—*This man is angry with you.* Look again.

Now—*This man just lost his wife.*

Look one last time.

Let yourself see that he is simply posing for a photo.

You felt that. Something *moved.*

You didn't see something new, but the experience changed. The space between you and him changed. What his face meant changed. How you felt looking at him changed.
What his silence meant.

It would be easy to explain this. To say you were given different interpretations...different stories...and your reaction followed. That sounds right. It even feels complete.

Stay with this for a second longer. Look at the photo again.
Try to look without changing anything.
Simply look.

Before you decide what you're seeing—notice what happens first.
Something lands.
A sensation. A tone. An interpretation.
It's already there...before you can name it.

The meaning doesn't wait for you. It arrives first.
Without warning.
And you experience through it.

Even now, as you're reading this—you're already doing it.

With these words.

With this page.

You're always doing it with whatever is in front of you.

You don't see meaning in things.

Meaning is what you see with.

And it changes everything you see.

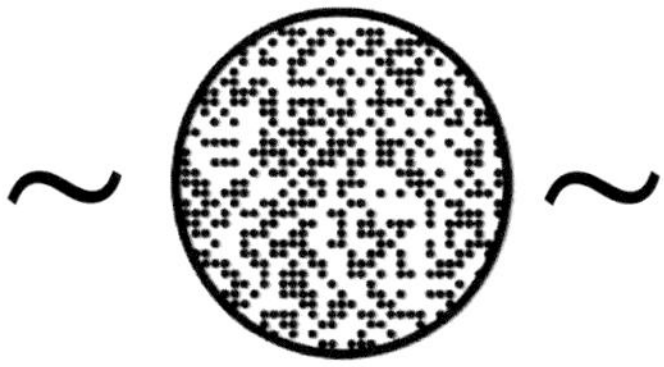

CHAPTER 6:

THAT'S NOT WHAT HAPPENED

Nothing about it feels uncertain.

A moment in a conversation...

You can replay something someone said. You can see where you were standing, hear the tone, feel what it meant. And it seems intact. Precise.

Try this.

Read the following list of words out loud.
Don't try to memorize them—just read.

Tired
Pillow
Dark
Rest
Yawn
Night
Blanket
Drowsy
Dream
Quiet
Soft
Comfortable

Now, look away from the page.

Without looking back, what words do you remember?
Take a moment and let them come.
Say them out loud to yourself.

Now, look at the list again.
One of the words you remembered...isn't there.
Sleep.
Bed.
They were never on the list.

Your brain didn't store the words, it stored the pattern—the shape of what they pointed to. And when you reached back in, it handed you the concept.

Fully formed.

Completely confident.

Wrong.

You didn't misremember words because you weren't paying attention.

You misremembered them because you were.

Your memory didn't fail.
It worked exactly as designed.
It just isn't doing what you thought it was doing.

And it isn't only words.

Think about a disagreement you've replayed in your mind more than once. You both remember it differently. Not because one of you is distorting events deliberately. Because you're each reaching back into a personal version that has been quietly reshaped every time you retrieved it.

What you felt the last time you remembered is now inside the memory itself. The version you're most certain of is the one you've revisited most often. Which means the memories that feel the most intact are also the most reconstructed.

The story you tell about what happened—in a relationship, in a defining moment, in your own history—is not a recording.

It's a living document.
Opened and quietly updated each time you return to it.
Shaped by who you are now, not who you were then.

Which means certainty isn't evidence of accuracy.

It's evidence of repetition.

CHAPTER 7:

THE LEVER

Dread is the right word for where you've arrived.

What you see isn't complete.

Where you are isn't fixed.

What you feel changes what stands out.

What you expect shapes what appears.

What you remember shifts over time.

What you experience isn't continuous.

If all of that is true—and now you've felt that it is—it raises something worse than a philosophical problem.

It raises a practical one.

If everything is being constructed, gaps filled in, quietly rewriting the past—

What can you actually do with that?

The honest answer is: more than you think.

Not everything moves.

There's something you've been using this entire time.
Something constant. Something so familiar you don't notice it.

Try this.

Look at whatever is in front of you.
Let your attention settle naturally on one thing.

Not the whole room. Just one thing.

Stay there for a few seconds.

Now—without moving your eyes—let your attention drop everything else.

Not by pushing it away.
Just stop including it.

Let the rest of the room fall out of importance.

Now shift.

Keep your eyes in the same place, but move your attention to something else in the room.

Not your gaze. Just your attention.

Go back. Then switch again.

What just happened?

The room didn't change.
But parts of it mattered less.

Then something else became the center.
Not gradually.
Immediately.

You didn't just notice something new.
You decided what was real enough to matter.
That wasn't perception.

That was choice.

That shift—is the lever.

You've been using it your entire life.

Constantly.

Without thinking about it.

When something stands out—your attention moves.
When something feels important—your attention locks in.
When something fades—your attention leaves.

And wherever it goes—your experience reorganizes around it.
Not all at once.
But enough to matter.

You don't experience everything equally.

You experience what you attend to.

Everything else doesn't disappear.

It just stops being you.

This has always been true. Even in the chapters before this.

When something disappeared—your attention wasn't there.

When time stretched—your attention arrived late.

When your sense of self shifted—your attention moved with it.

It's been the common thread.

The whole time.

You don't control everything. But you're not without influence.

You can't stop prediction.
You can't stop emotion.
You can't stop memory from shifting.

But you can place your attention.

And where you place it—changes what stabilizes.
Changes what strengthens.
Changes what becomes your experience.

You don't need to control the whole system. You only need to control the entry point.

And this is it.

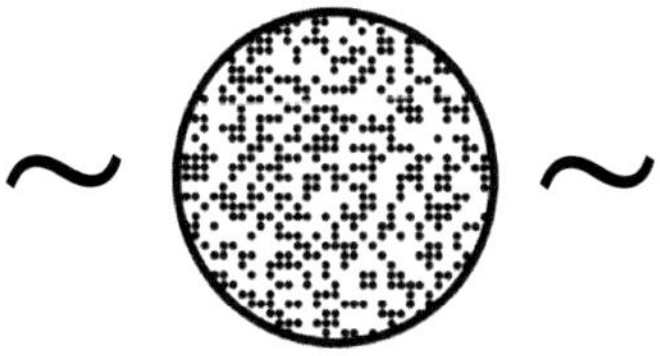

CHAPTER 8:

HOLD IT

You know where the lever is. But knowing it exists...and being able to use it—are not the same thing.

Try this.

Pick something simple.

A word on this page.

A point in the room.

The feeling in your hand.

Place your attention there. And hold it.
Not rigidly.
Just...keep it there.

For a few seconds, it's easy. Clear. Stable.

And then—something happens.

A thought appears. A sensation shifts. Something pulls.
And without deciding to—your attention moves.

You notice it after. Not during.
And by the time you notice—you're already somewhere else.
You didn't choose to leave. You were just gone.

Bring it back. Hold it again. Same thing. It drifts.

Not because you chose to move it.
Because the system is designed to respond.
To novelty. To relevance. To emotion. To unfinished patterns.
Your attention isn't weak. It's active.

But it isn't stable.
And because it isn't stable, your experience isn't stable.
Whatever captures your attention, captures your **reality**.

Even briefly.

A single thought can pull you into a different state.

A single sensation can redirect your focus.

A single memory can shift how everything feels.

Instantly.

Because the moment attention moves—the system reorganizes.
And most of the time—this is happening without you.
But not always.

There's a difference between attention being pulled...
and attention being placed.
You've already felt it. In the last chapter.

Now you're seeing the gap.
The gap is the moment you notice it's already gone.
That's the only place control actually exists.

Right now, your attention moves more than you do.
But that can change.
Not by forcing it. Not by locking it down.
By returning it.
Again.
And again.
And again.
Each time it drifts—and you notice—and you bring it back—
something strengthens.

Subtle.

But real.

The movement becomes clearer.
The return becomes faster.
The placement becomes more precise.

You don't stop the system.
You start working with it.

And over time—something new begins to happen.
Attention doesn't just land. It stays.
Not perfectly. But longer.

Long enough to stabilize what you're experiencing.
Long enough to influence what develops.
Long enough to matter.

This is where it stops being automatic.

And starts becoming a skill.

~ ~

CHAPTER 9:
TURN IT UP

Once you can place it—it becomes obvious that attention isn't neutral.

It doesn't just land somewhere and observe. It participates.
It feels whatever it touches—and what it touches changes.
Not slowly. Immediately.

Try this.

Find something neutral. Something simple.
A sound in the room. The feeling of your breath. The weight of your body where you're sitting. Place your attention there.
Hold it—just long enough to feel it clearly.
And while you're there—notice what happens to everything else.

It doesn't disappear. But it drops. Softens. Loses its edge.
Not because it changed.
Because you stopped feeding it.

Now shift.

Bring your attention to something slightly uncomfortable.
A tension in your body. A lingering thought.
Something unfinished.

Place your attention there.
Stay.
Notice what happens.

It sharpens.

It becomes harder to ignore.

More present. More real.

If you stay long enough—it starts to pull.

Not dramatically. Just steadily.

Like it has more weight than it did a moment ago.
Like it was always this heavy. You didn't make it heavier.

You just kept looking.

Same system. Same world.
Different placement. Different result.

That's not a small thing.

And it isn't optional.

Attention amplifies.

Not sometimes. Always. Even when you wish it wouldn't.
Whatever you attend to becomes more prominent.
What you ignore fades.

This has always been happening. In every version of yourself you've inhabited. You weren't choosing randomly.
But you weren't choosing deliberately either.

Now you are.

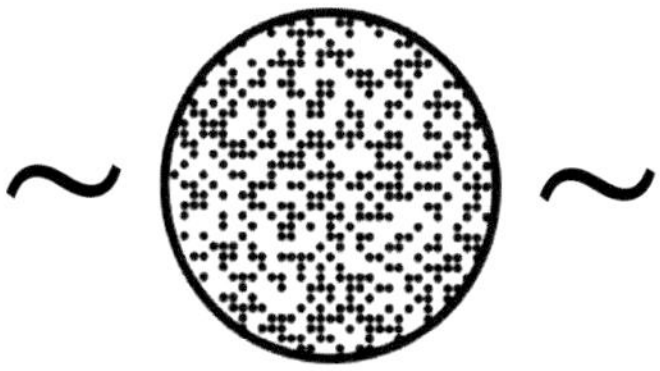

CHAPTER 10:
THAT'S IT

Under your awareness, you've been doing this the entire time.
Things disappeared.
Time stretched.
Your sense of where you are shifted.
What you expected shaped what appeared.
How you felt changed what stood out.
What you remember changed each time you reached for it.
None of that was theoretical.
You experienced it.

Which means something simple is no longer avoidable.
What you experience is not just happening.
It's being formed.
Moment by moment.

Most of it runs automatically.
But not all of it.
There is a point where you can enter the process.

Not to control everything.
Not to force outcomes.
But to influence what stabilizes.

You've already found it.

Where your attention goes—your experience begins to organize.
Not instantly. Not completely.
But enough to matter.

What you attend to more often becomes clearer.
More familiar.
More real.

What you stop attending to fades.

Not because it's gone.
Because it's no longer being reinforced.

Which means reality is not something you're passively receiving.
It's something you're participating in.

And if that's true—then the question is no longer:

"What is real?"

The question is:

"What are you practicing?"

Because whatever you practice—becomes easier.

Becomes automatic.
Becomes what feels natural.
And eventually—becomes what feels real.

You don't need new perception.

You need refined contact with the one you already have.

Don't do anything yet.

Just sit for a moment and wait for your next thought.

Not forcing it.

Not chasing it.

Just...wait...

You don't know what it's going to be.

You can't predict it. You can't see it coming.

And yet—it arrives. Fully formed.

Look at that carefully.

If you don't know what's about to appear—what exactly are you standing on?

Just notice what it does to the way you're sitting here.

About the Author

Oliver studied at Virginia Military Institute (VMI) in Lexington, Virginia, and at the University of Paris IV—La Sorbonne in Paris, France. He lives and works at the edges of human experience: emergency medicine, skydiving, and the quiet architecture of attention.

Made in the USA
Coppell, TX
07 July 2026

84326301R00038